Asshole

An Irreverent Adult Coloring Book

For Release Anger

By

S.B. Nozaz

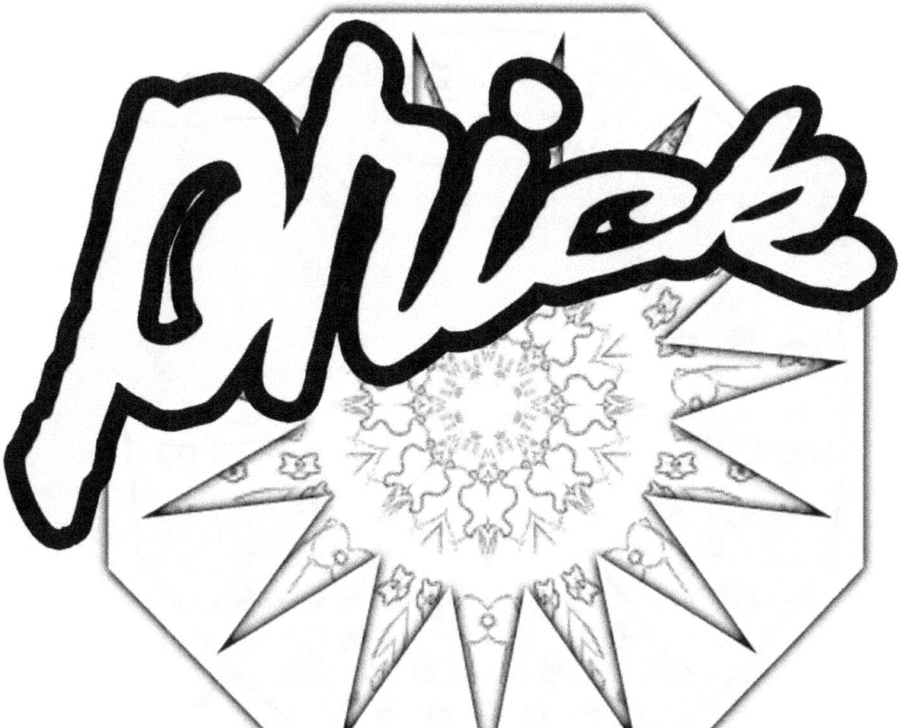

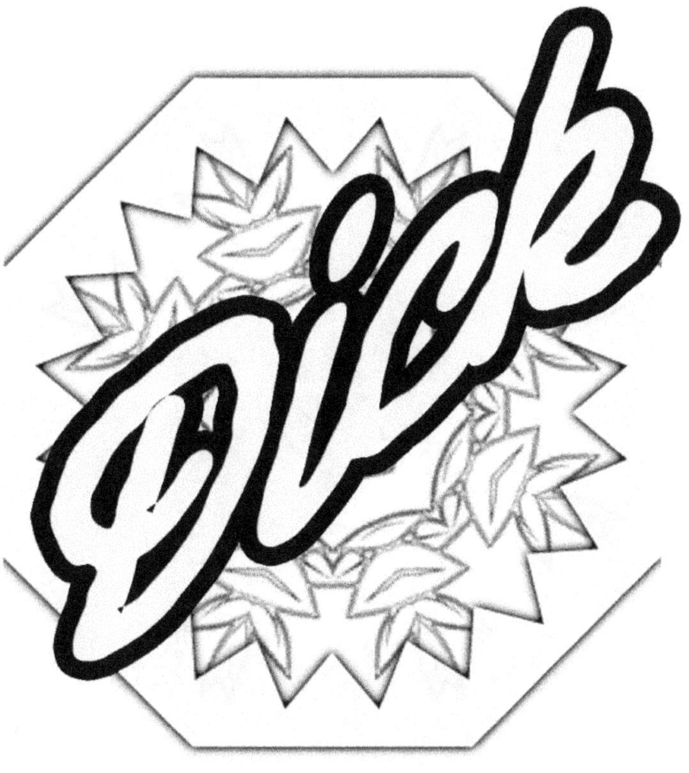
Dick

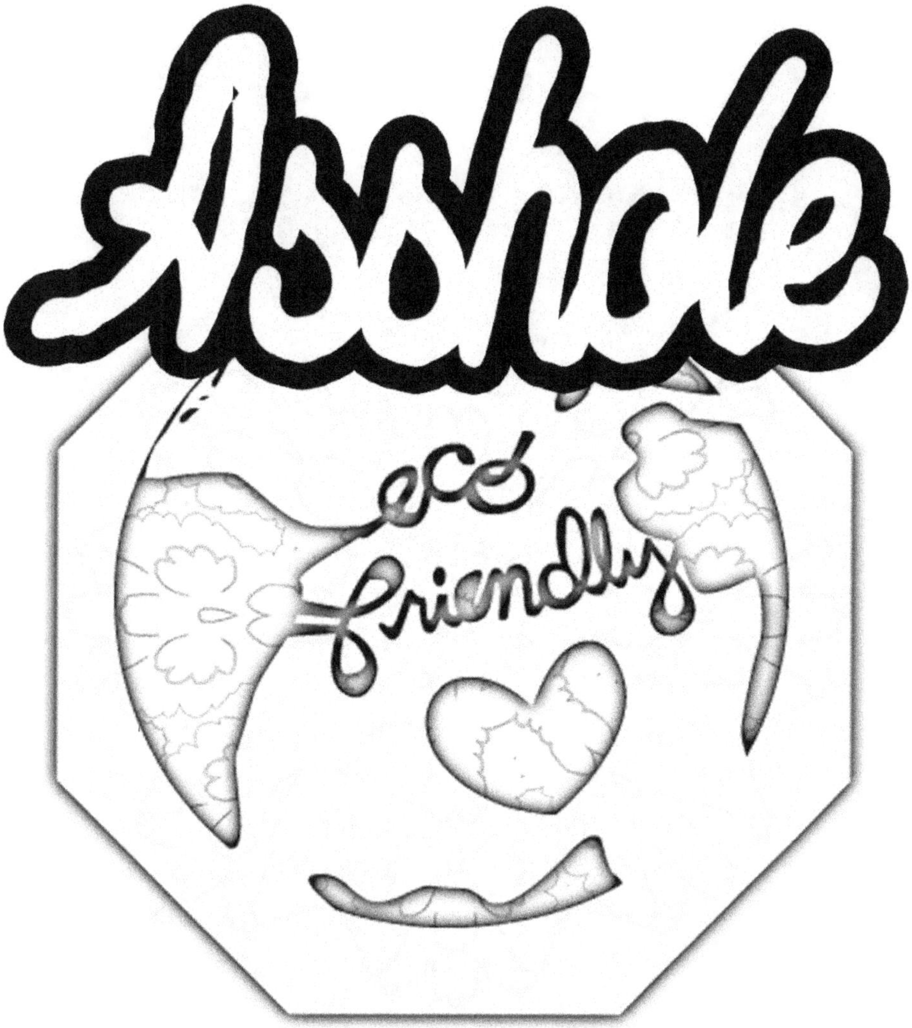
Asshole
eco friendly

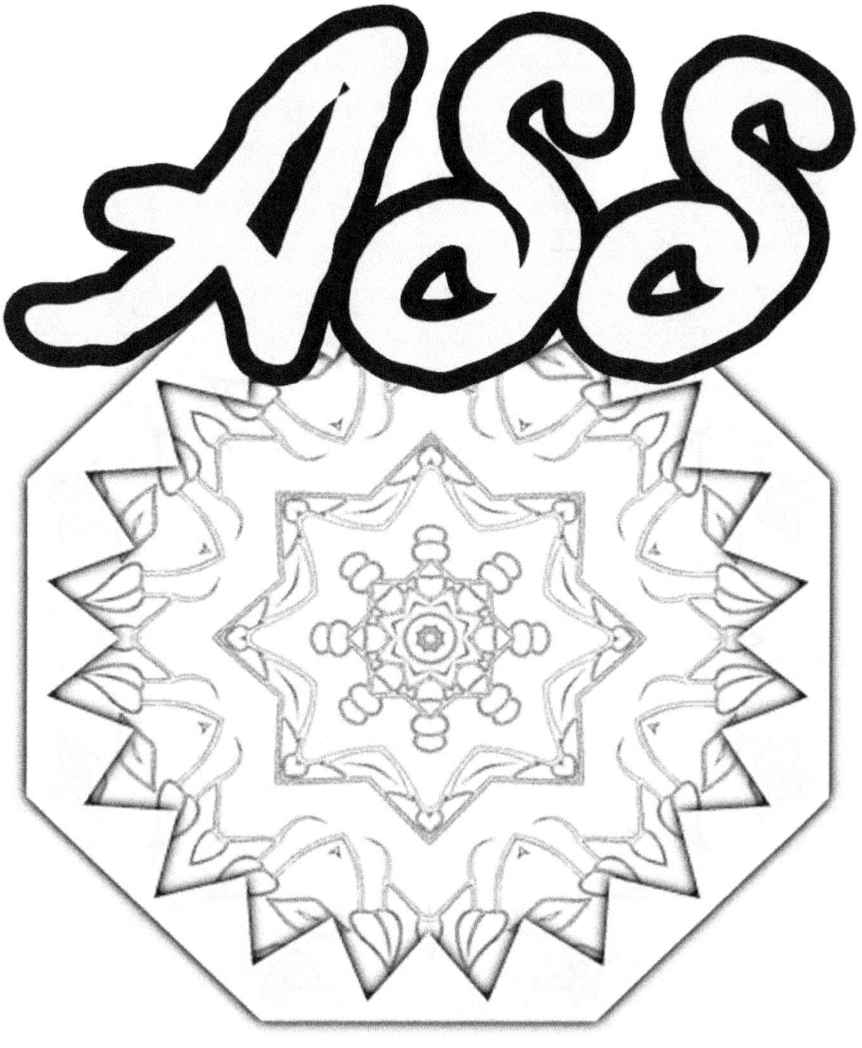

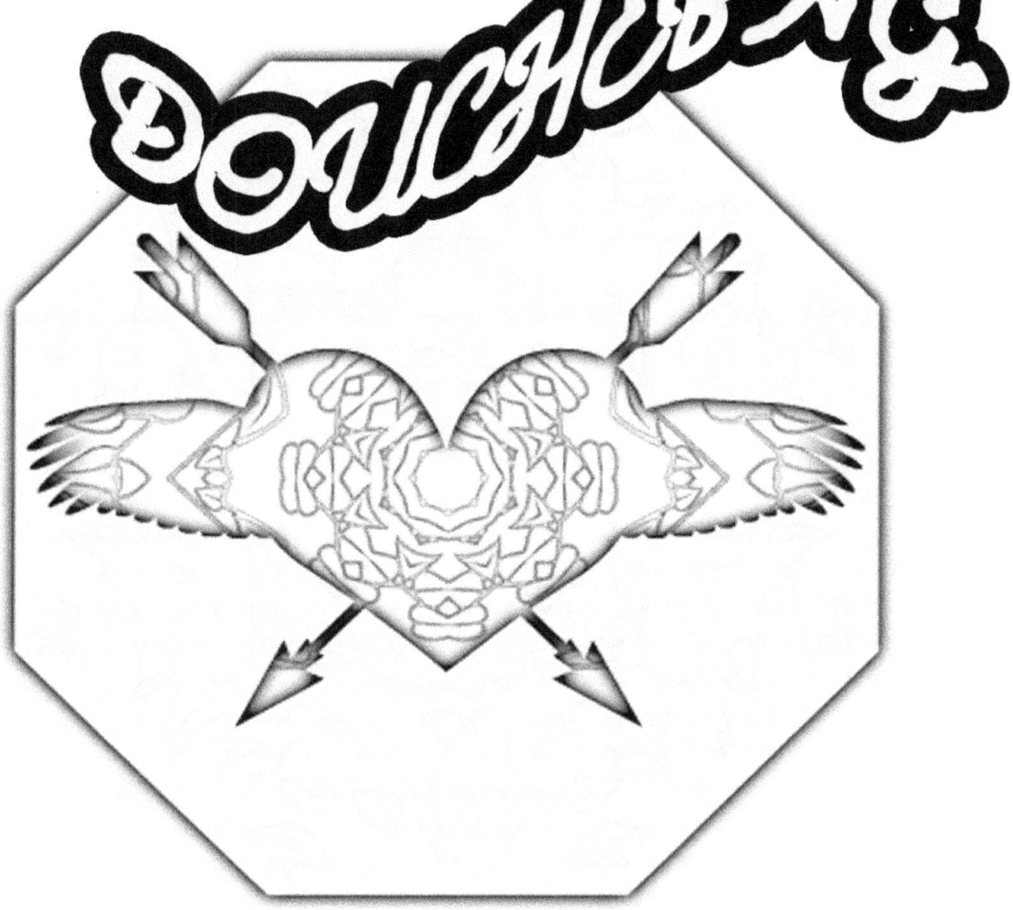
DOUCHEBAG

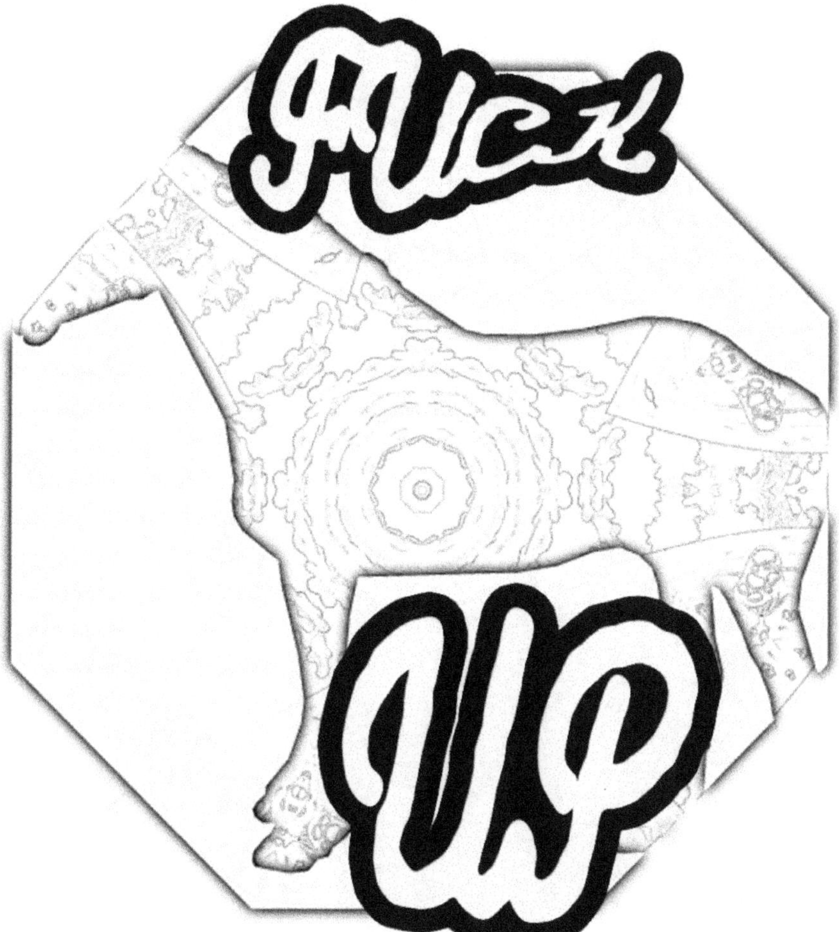
Fuck
UP

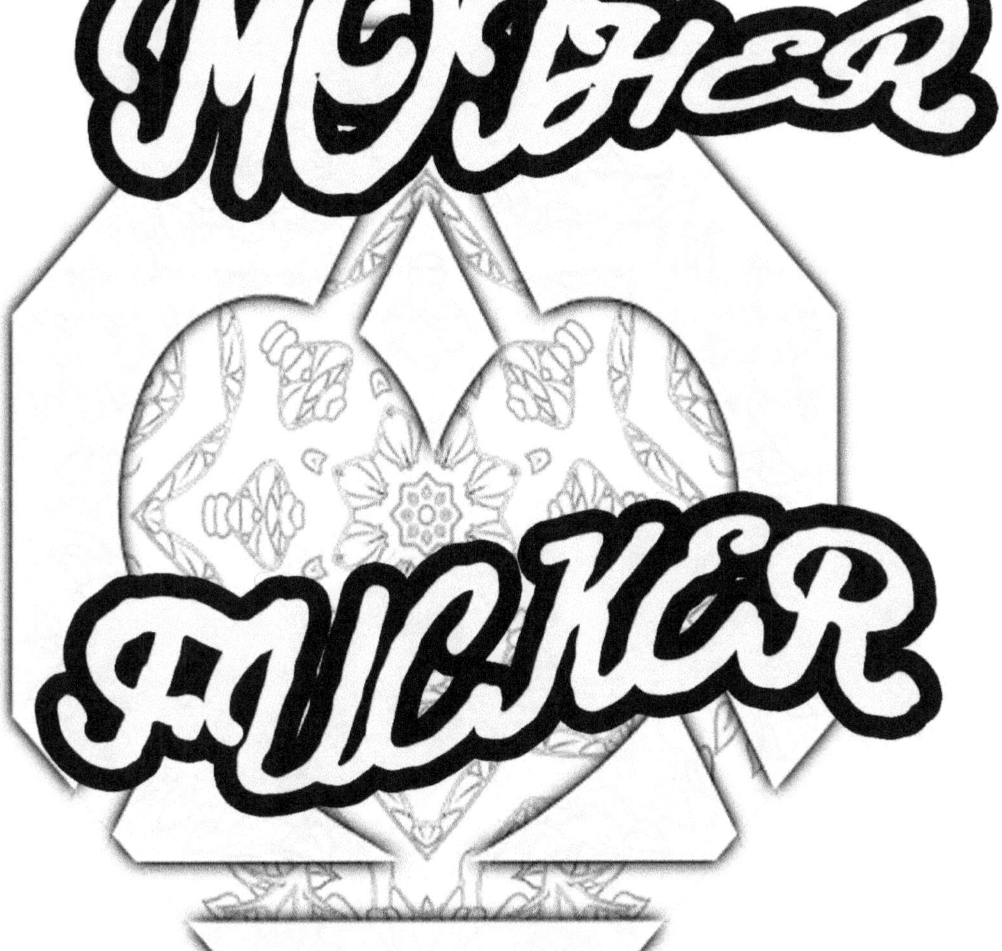
MOTHER
FUCKER

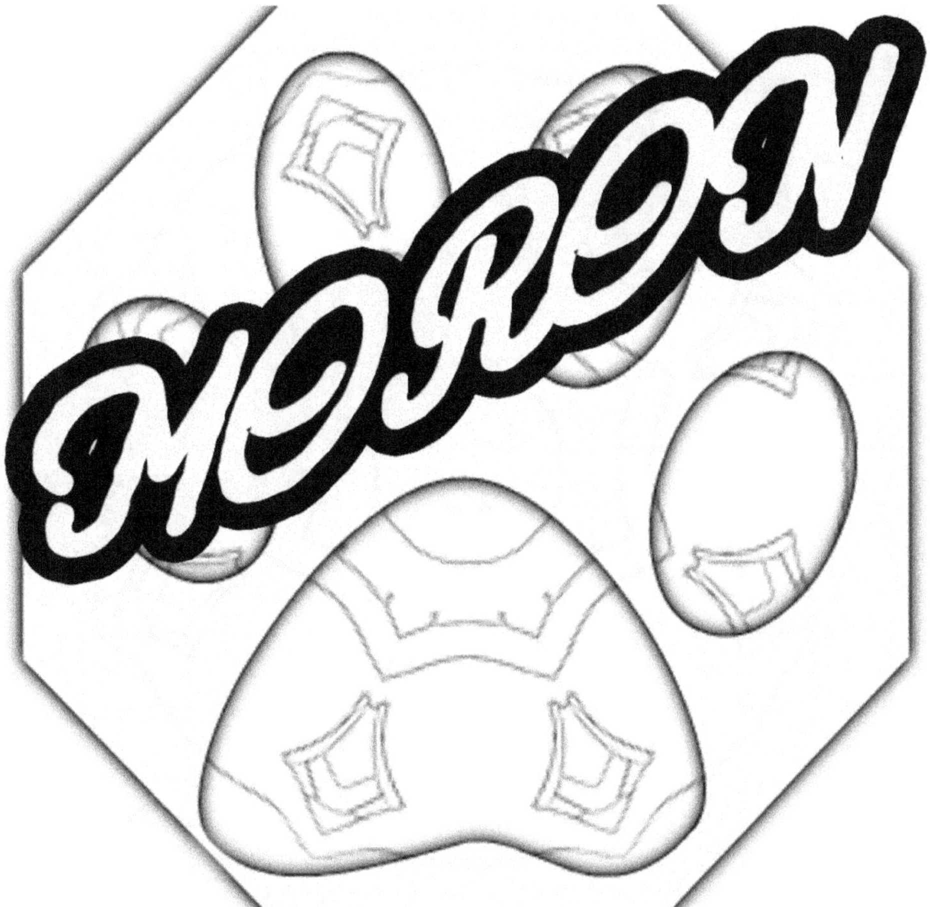
MORON

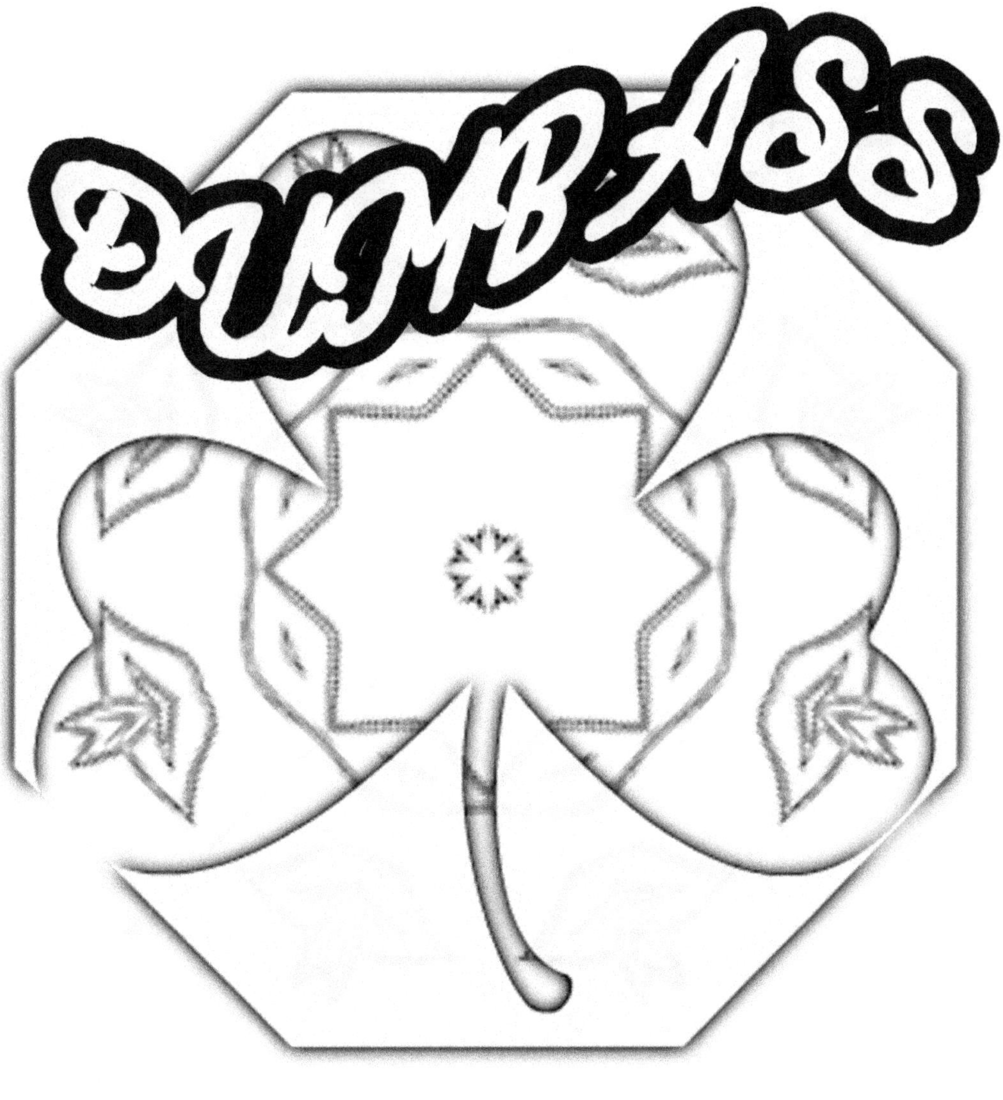
DUMBASS

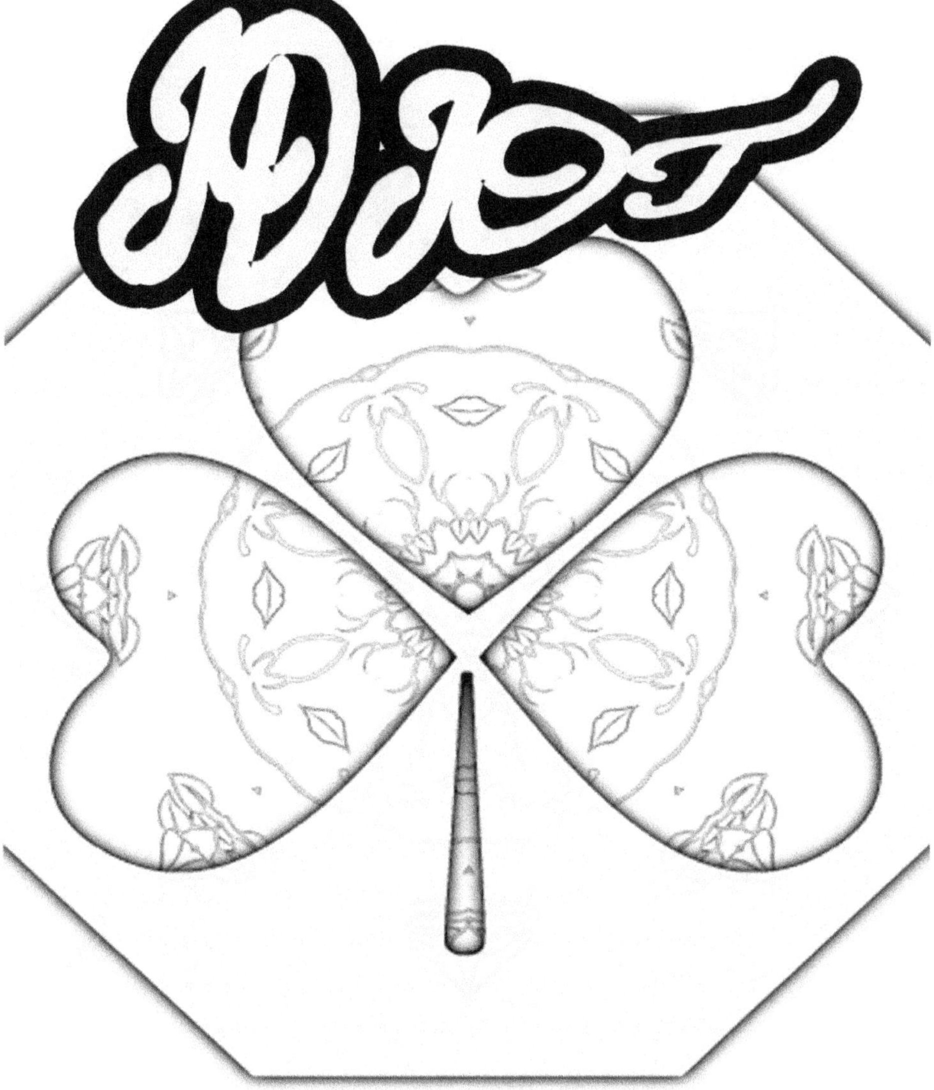

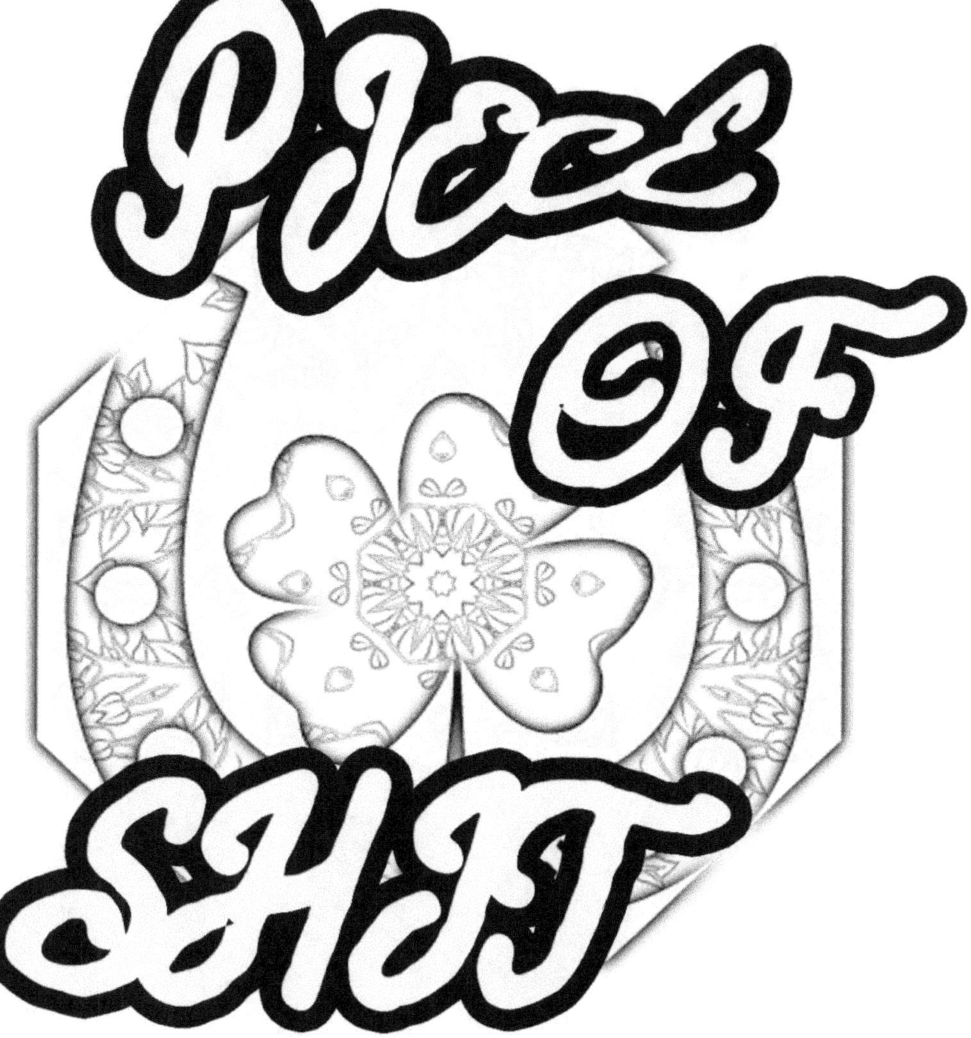
Piece
OF
SHIT

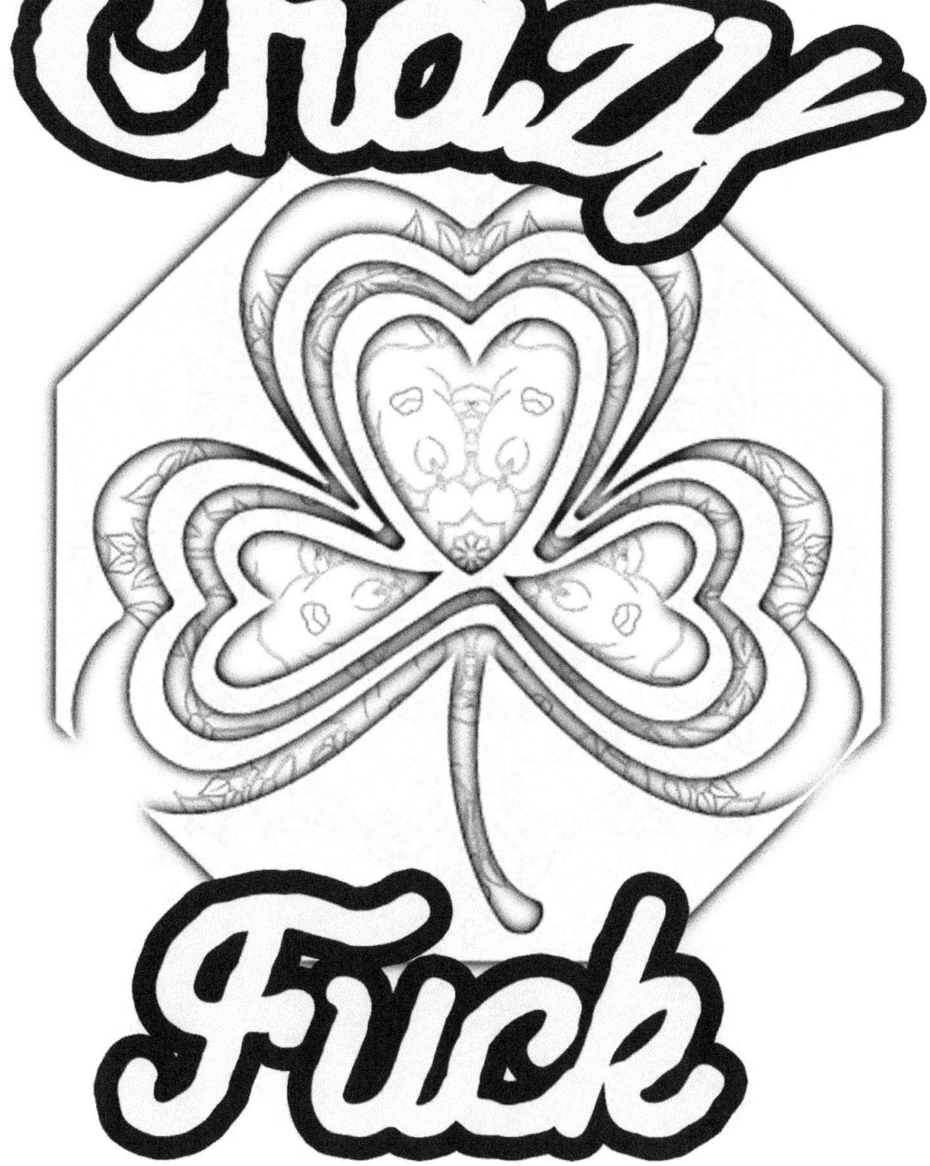
Crazy
Fuck

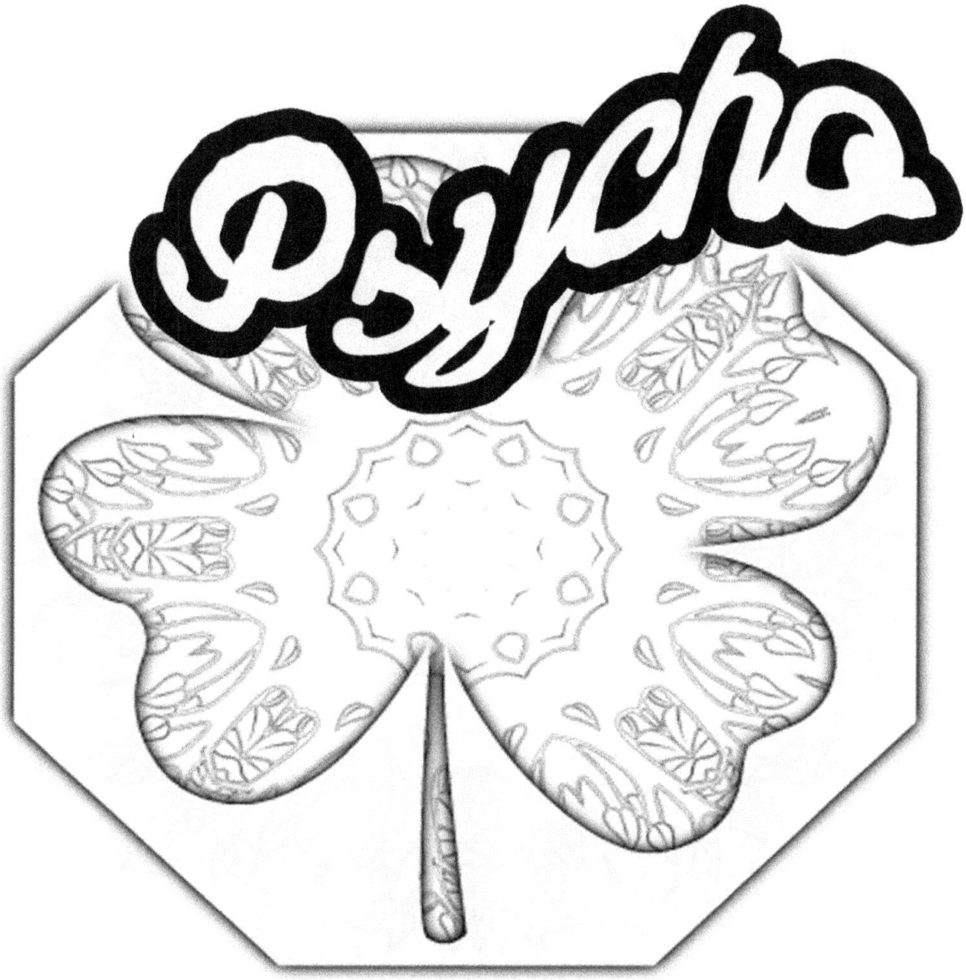
Psycho

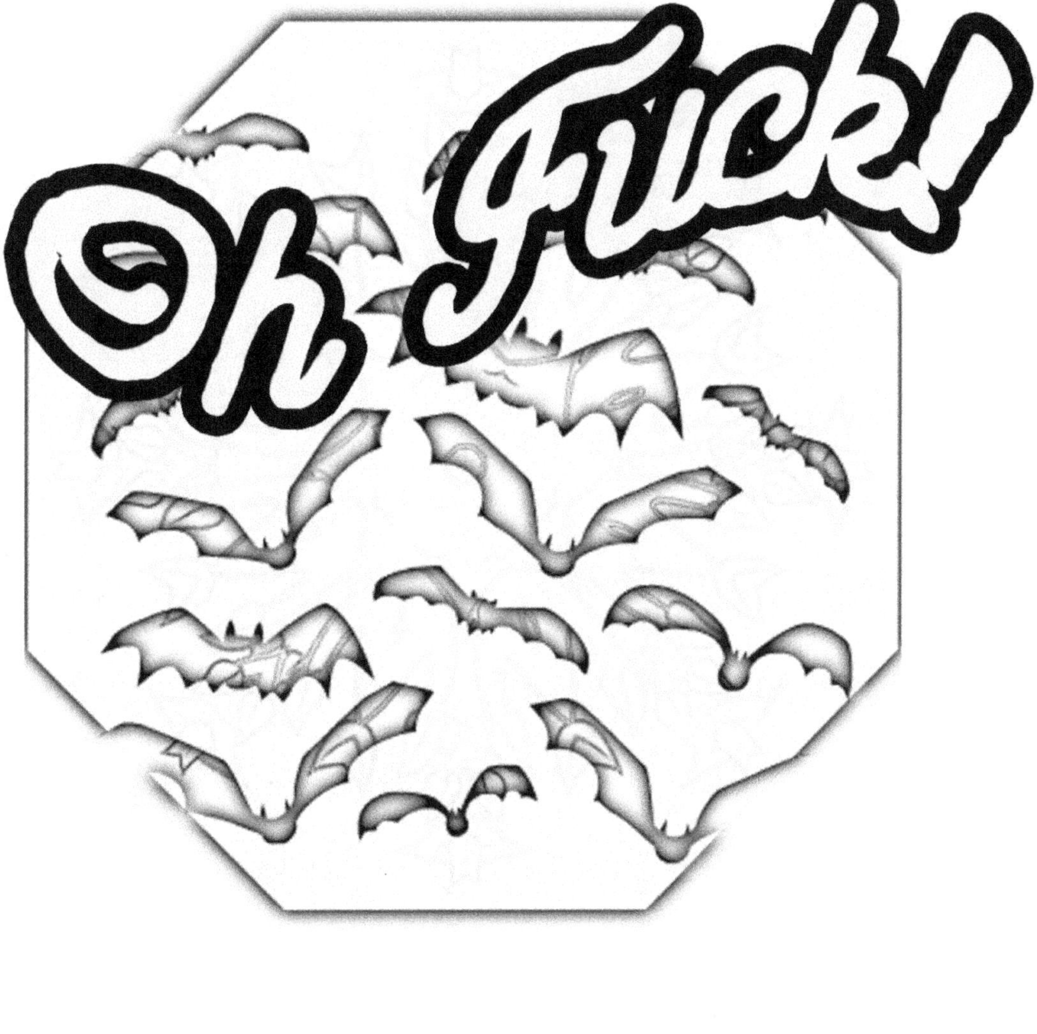
Oh Fuck!

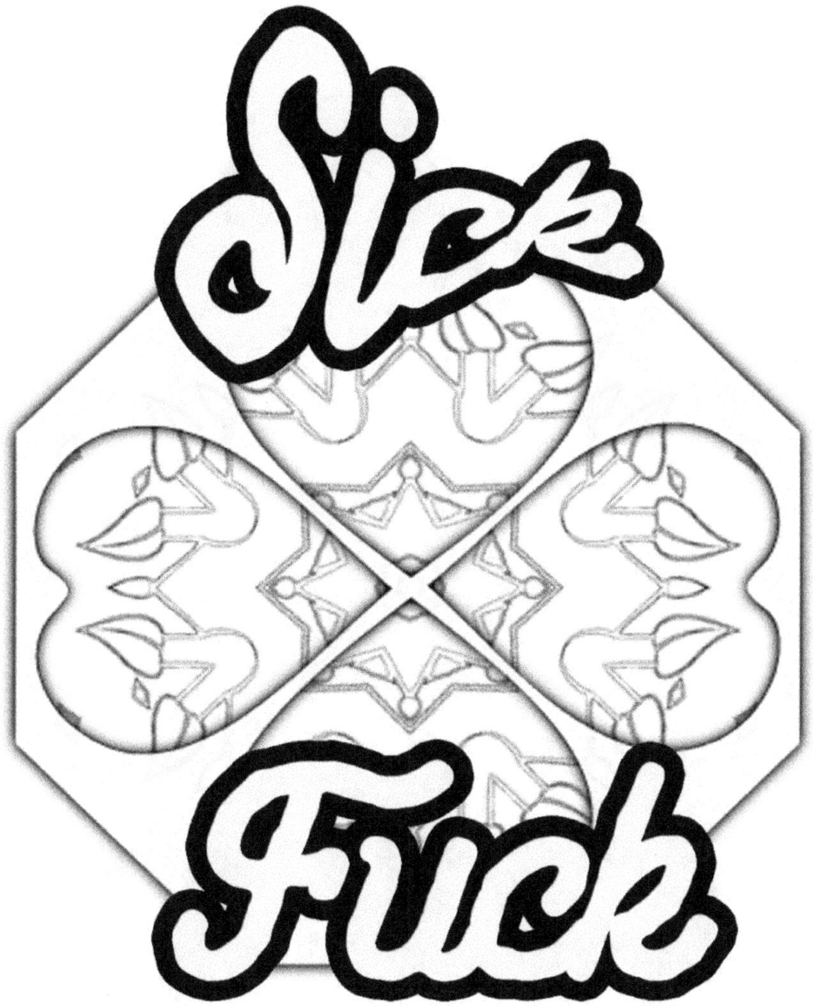
Sick
Fuck

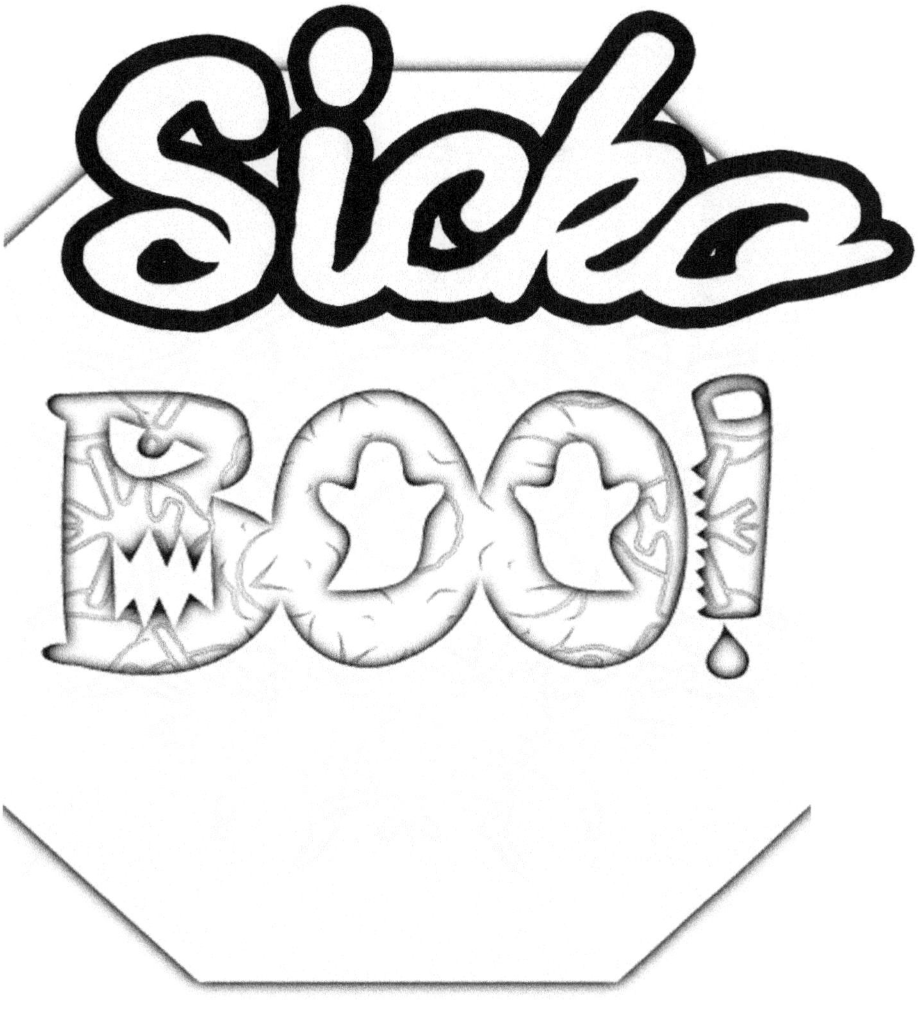
Sicko
BOO!

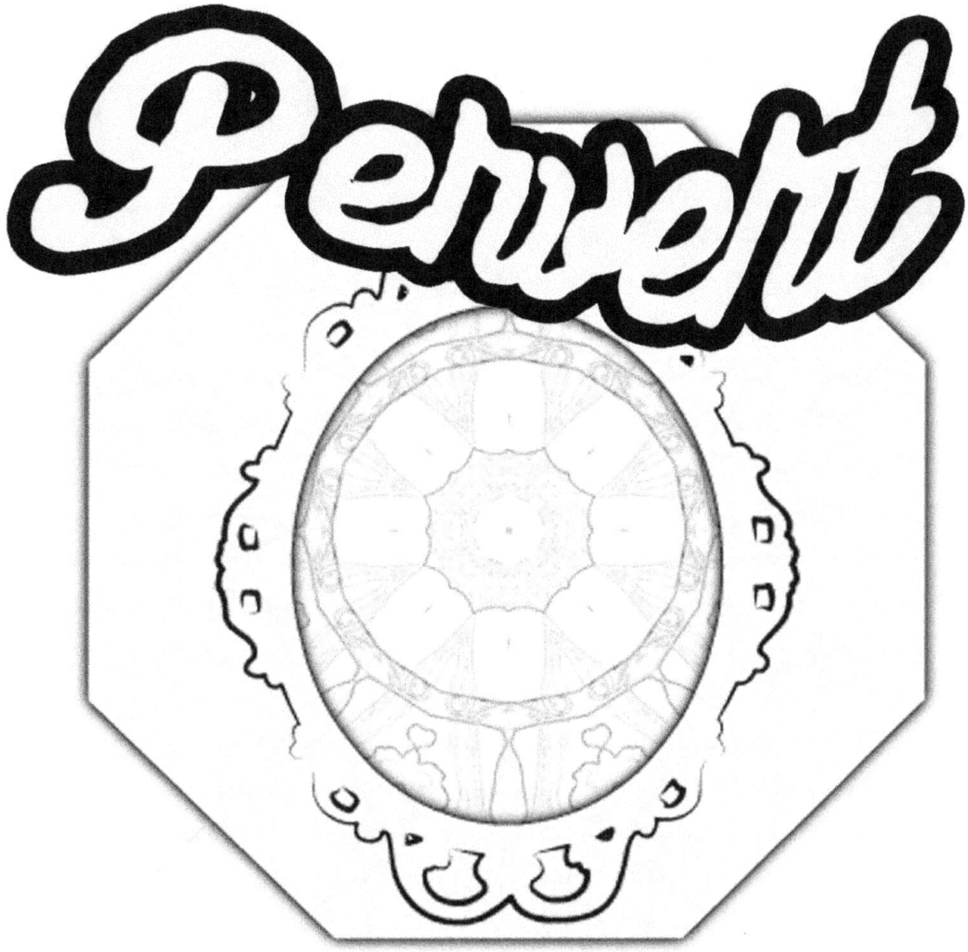
Pervert

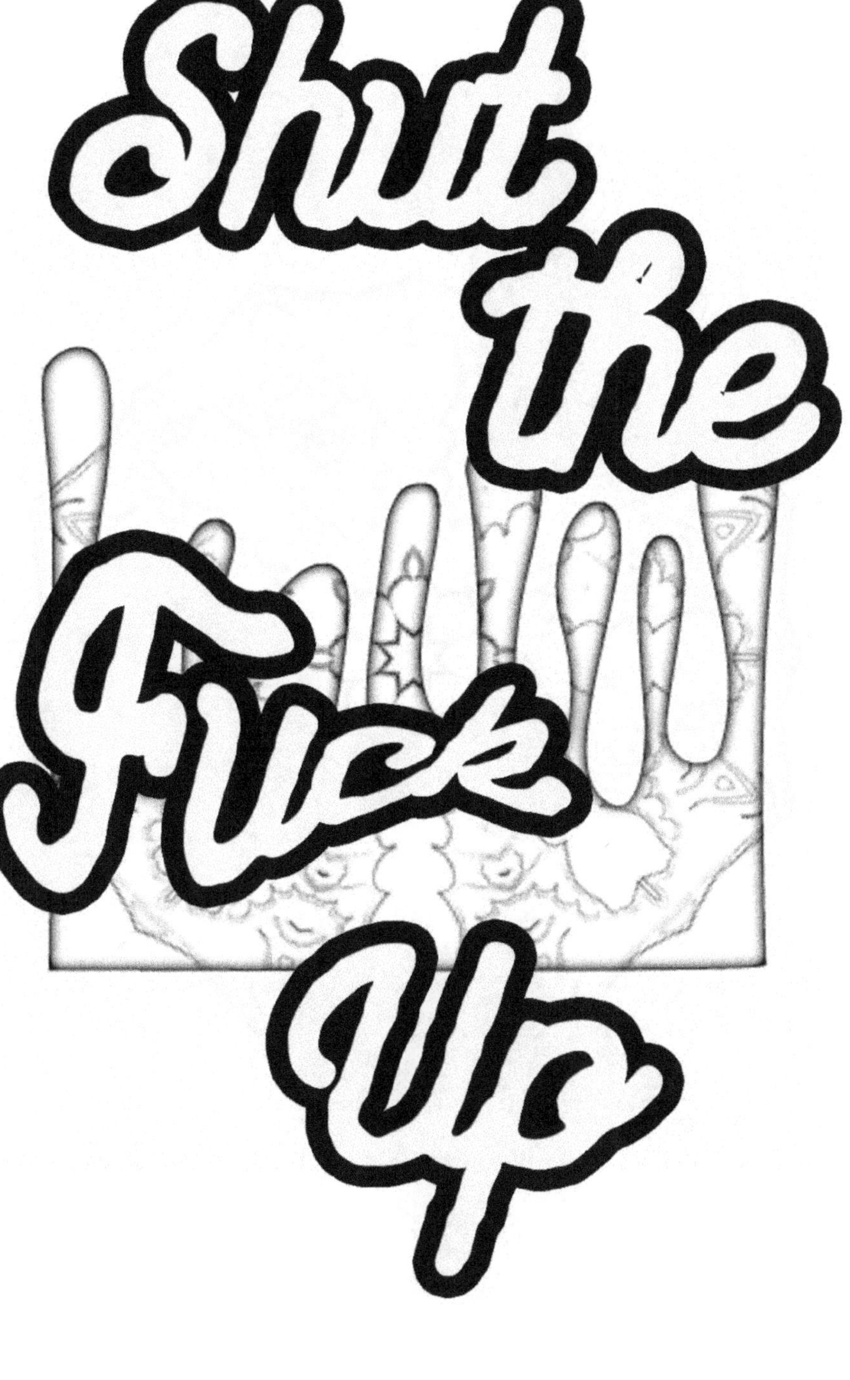
Shut
the
Fuck
Up

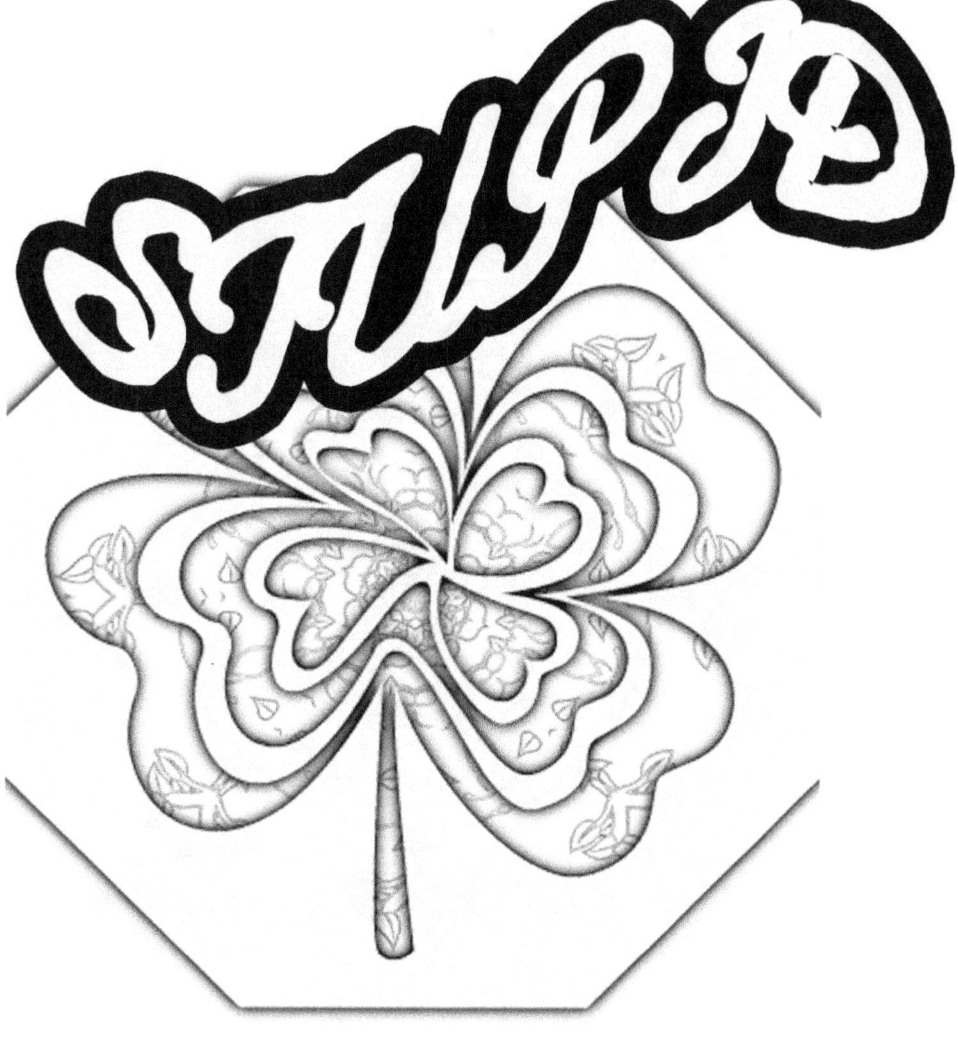

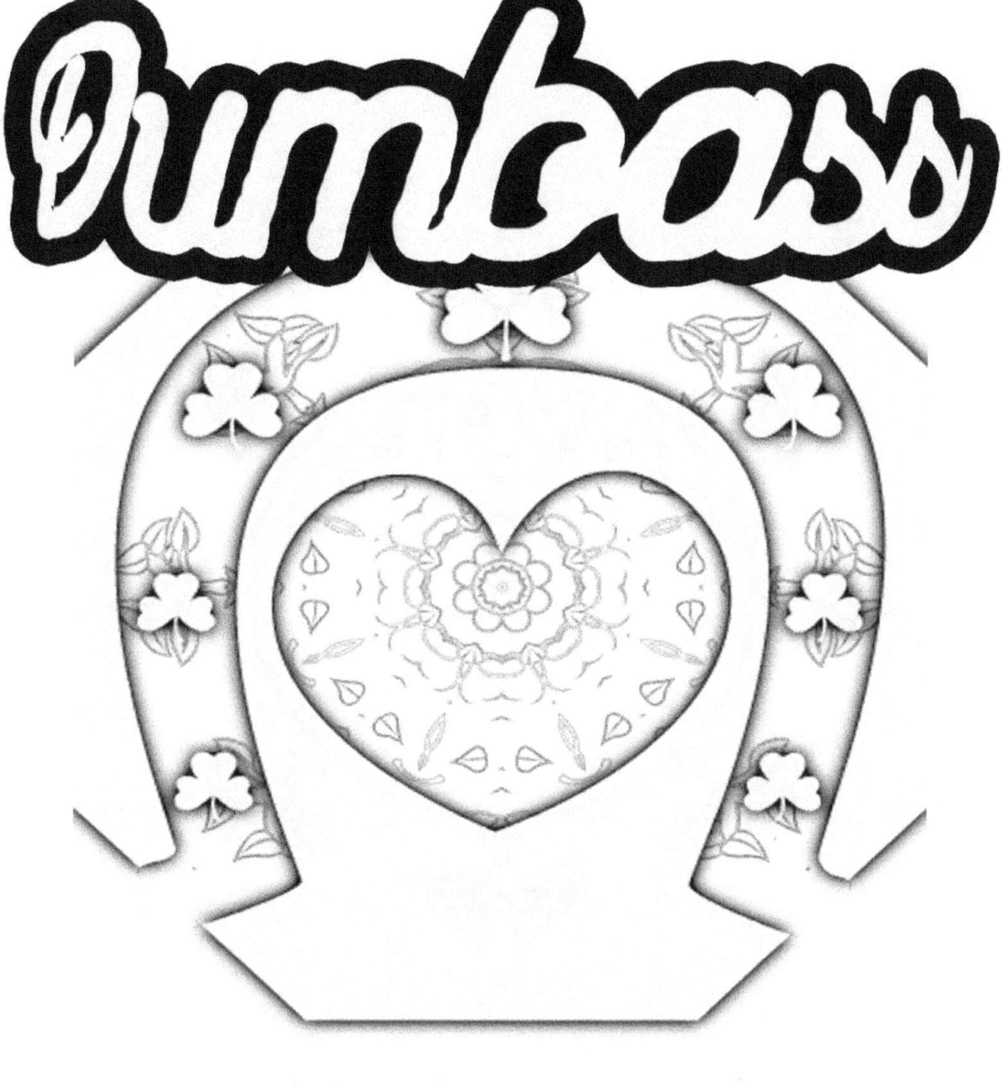
Dumbass

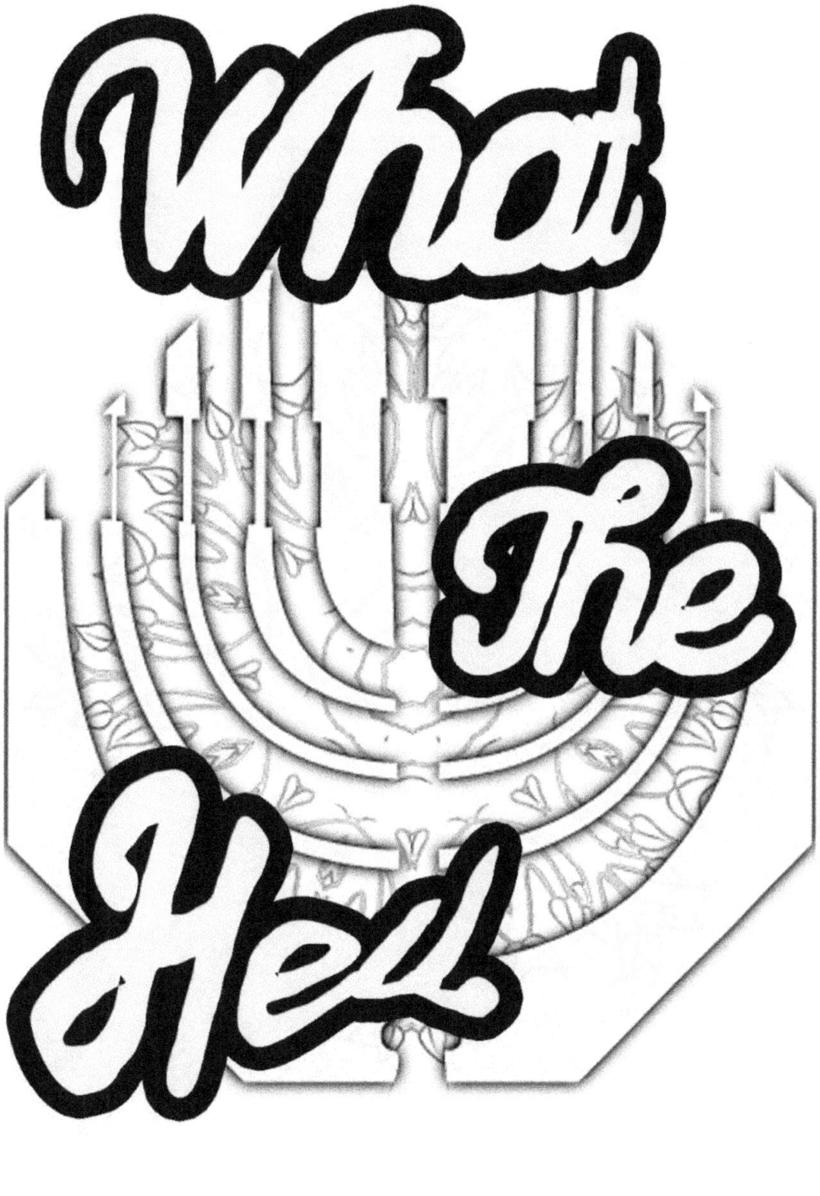
What
The
Hell

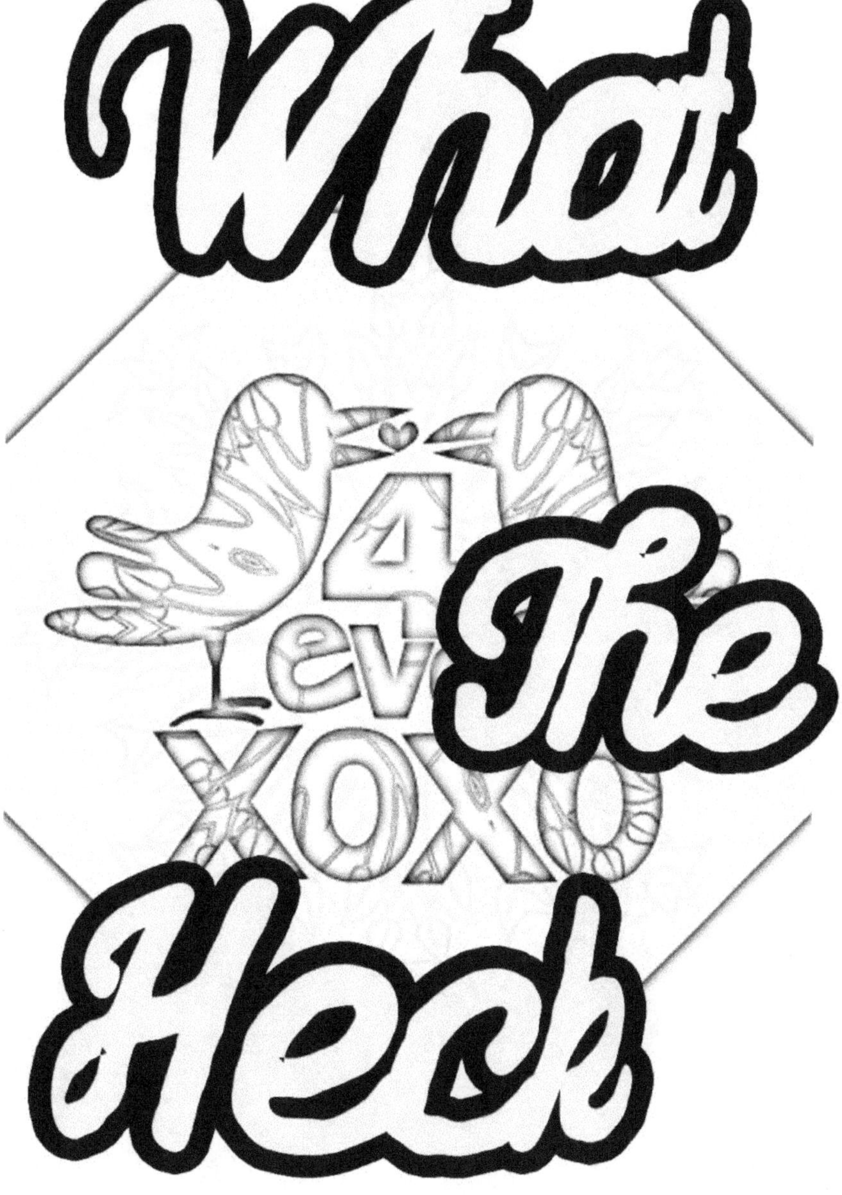
What
The
Heck
4
XOXO

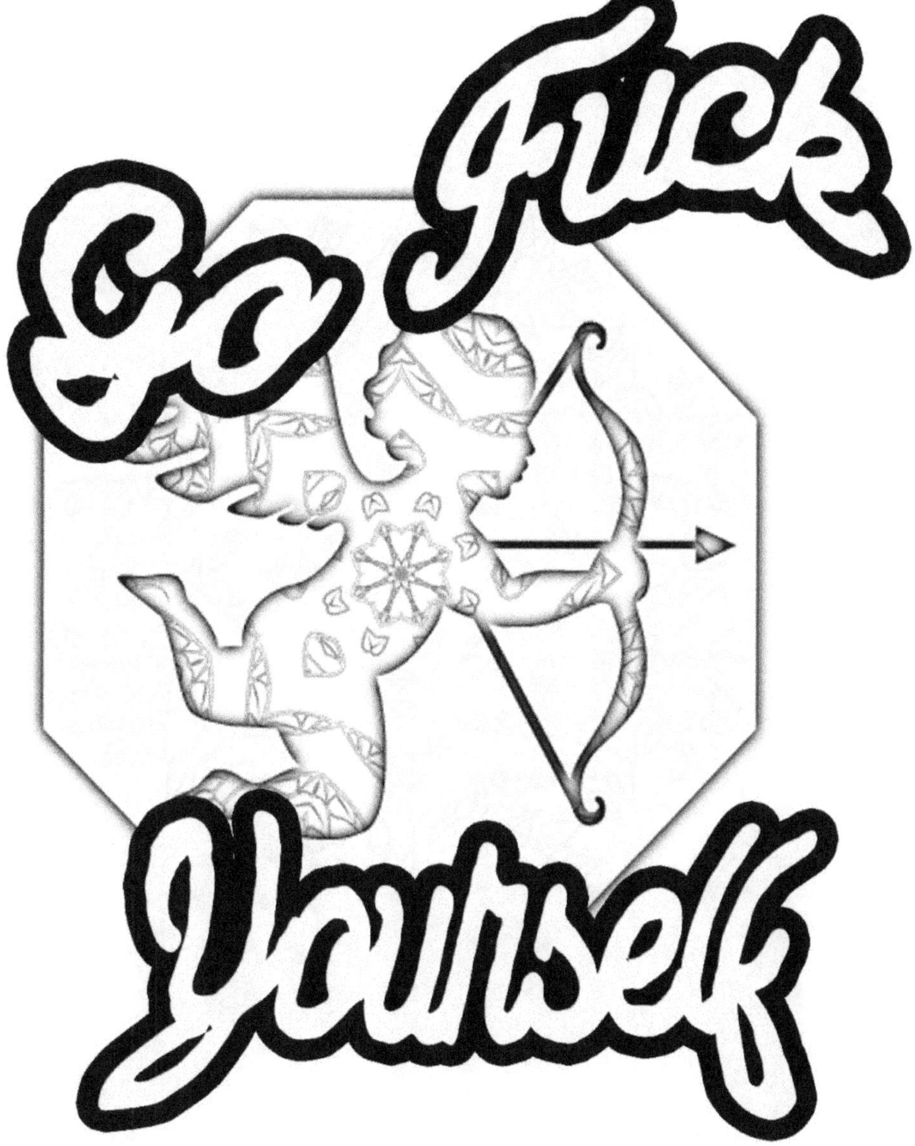
Go Fuck
Yourself

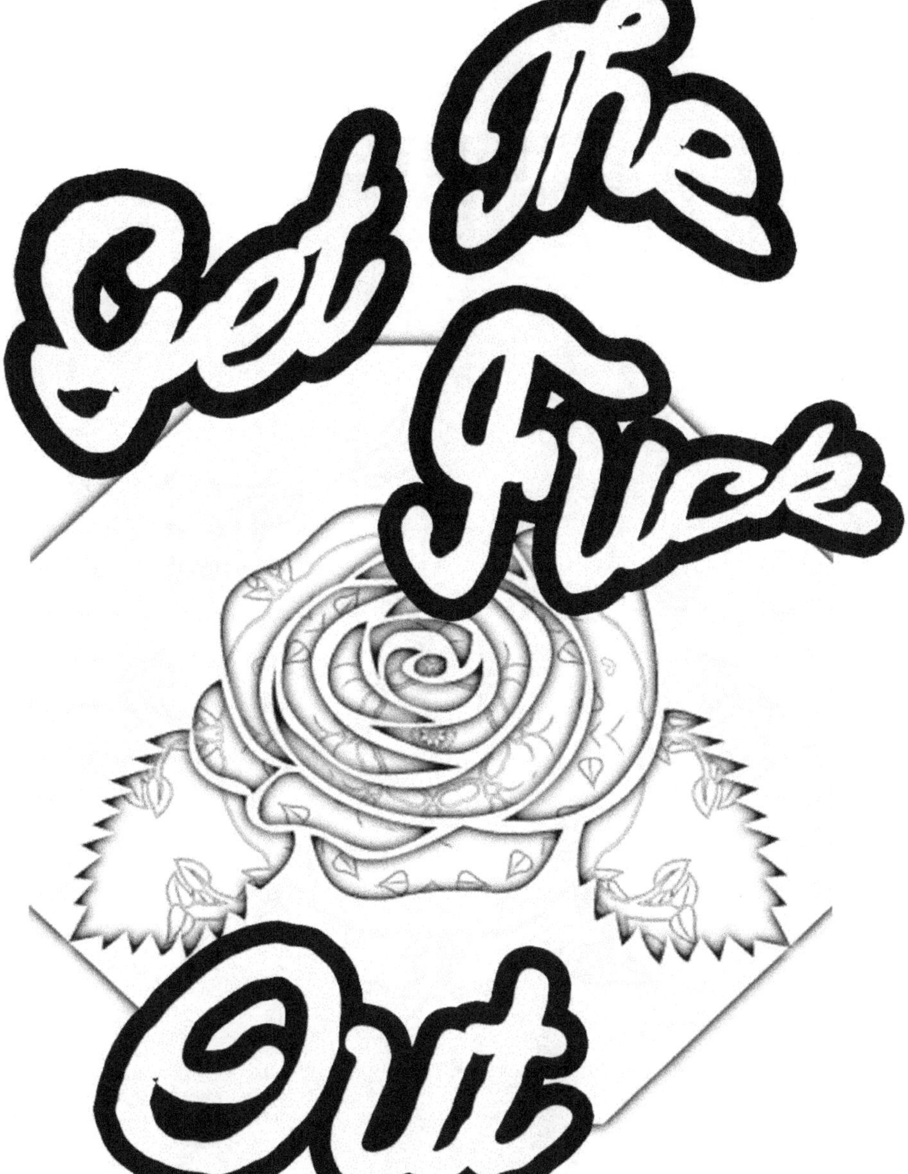

Get The
Fuck
Out

Note

www.ingramcontent.com/pod-product-compliance
Lightning Source LLC
Chambersburg PA
CBHW080635190526
45169CB00009B/3398